Romans

Teaching Tips

Purple Level 8

This book focuses on the grapheme /ie/.

Before Reading
- Discuss the title. Ask readers what they think the book will be about. Have them support their answer.
- Discuss the book's focused grapheme: /ie/. Explain that it has two main sounds: long /i/ and long /e/. Give examples of each, such as *pie* and *shield*.

Read the Book
- Encourage readers to read independently, either aloud or silently to themselves.
- Prompt readers to break down unfamiliar words into units of sound and string the sounds together to form the words. Then, ask them to look for context clues to see if they can figure out what these words mean. Discuss new vocabulary to confirm meaning.
- Urge readers to point out when the focused phonics grapheme appears in the text. What sound is it making?

After Reading
- Ask readers comprehension questions about the book. What did you learn about Roman armies in this book? What more would you like to learn about the Romans?
- Encourage readers to think of words with the /ie/ grapheme. On a separate sheet of paper, have them write the words. Group them by the different /ie/ sounds.

© 2024 Booklife Publishing
This edition is published by arrangement with Booklife Publishing.

North American adaptations © 2024 Jump!
5357 Penn Avenue South
Minneapolis, MN 55419
www.jumplibrary.com

Decodables by Jump! are published by Jump! Library.
All rights reserved. No part of this book may be reproduced in any form without written permission from the publisher.

Library of Congress Cataloging-in-Publication Data is available at www.loc.gov or upon request from the publisher.

ISBN: 979-8-88524-787-0 (hardcover)
ISBN: 979-8-88524-788-7 (paperback)
ISBN: 979-8-88524-789-4 (ebook)

Photo Credits

Images are courtesy of Shutterstock.com. Cover, p4–5 – Alfmaler, BudOlga. p3 – photolinc, Photosampler, Pixel-Shot. p6–7 – leoks, AlexZaitsev. p8–9 – Deatonphotos, meunierd. p10–11 – meunierd, Sergej Razvodovskij. p12–13 – Maljalen, Massimo Todaro. p14–15 – WindVector, Artem Mishukov. p16 – Shutterstock.

Which of these things has a name with **ie** in it?

Ancient Romans lived more than 2,000 years ago and lived all around the planet. We can still see evidence of this now, such as the aqueducts.

The Romans were good at making lots of things, such as roads. Lots of the things they made are still around now.

Roman roads can still be found around the globe.

The Roman Empire had strong armies. They trained hard to become good at fighting. When they defeated other armies, those armies joined the Roman Empire.

The Roman armies had better equipment than other armies at the time. Their equipment and their training gave them the upper hand in fights.

The Romans had better shields than most other armies that they met. They used them along with other shields in a big team to defend themselves from arrows.

The shields were made to fit with other shields without gaps. When using their shields like this, the Romans could move across a field raining with arrows without getting hit.

The Romans had lots of gods, and they all did different things. There was a goddess of harvest. Romans prayed to her and asked for good food to grow in the fields.

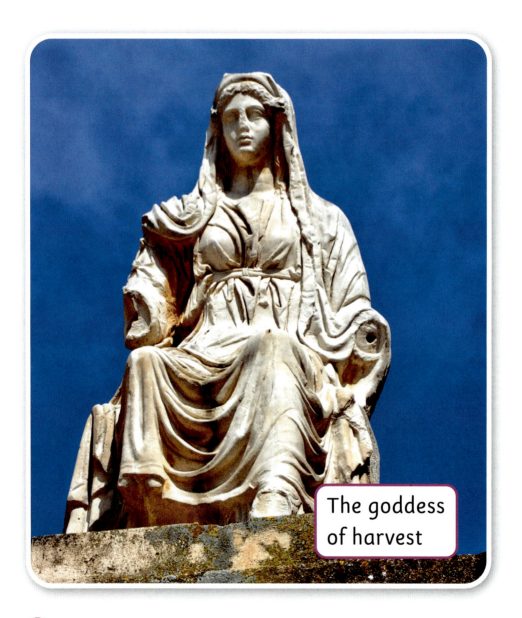

The goddess of harvest

The Romans gave offerings to the gods. They believed that if they did this, the god or goddess might help them. Some offerings were grapes or grain.

Laverna was the Roman goddess of thieves and mischief. The Romans used to believe that she spent all her time tricking the people in the Roman Empire.

Thieves were often punished in Rome. They might have had to pay back more coins than they had stolen. Some thieves were killed as a warning to other thieves.

The Romans liked to go to the amphitheater. It was an open-air arena where lots of events were held. Crowds watched races and fights there.

An emperor ruled the Roman Empire. The emperor was the highest power in the land. He could make rules and told the armies what to do and where to go.

Say the name of each object below. Is the "ie" in each a long /e/ sound or a long /i/ sound?

cookie

tie

pie

field